THE PSYCHEDELICS

COLORING BOOK

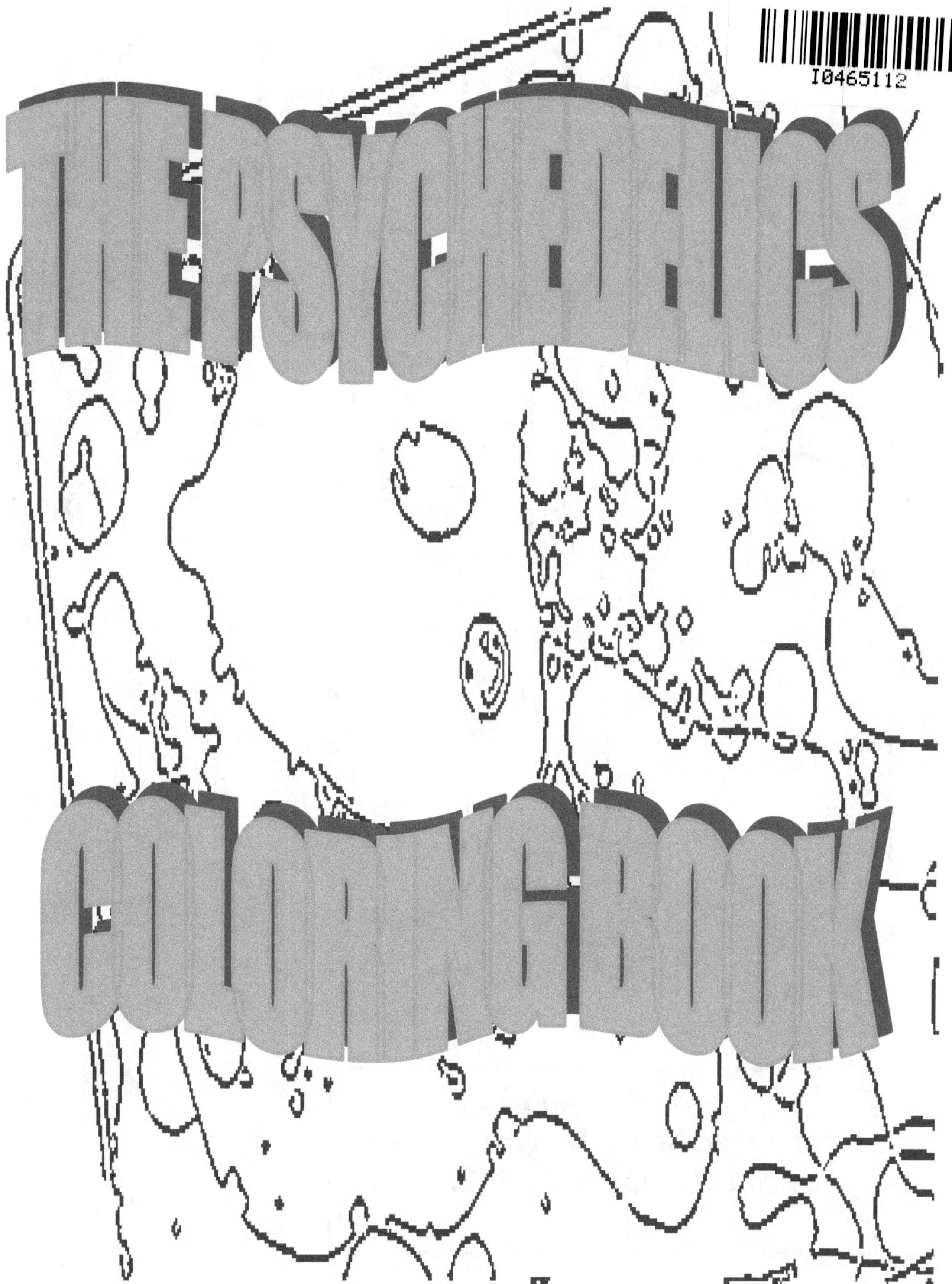

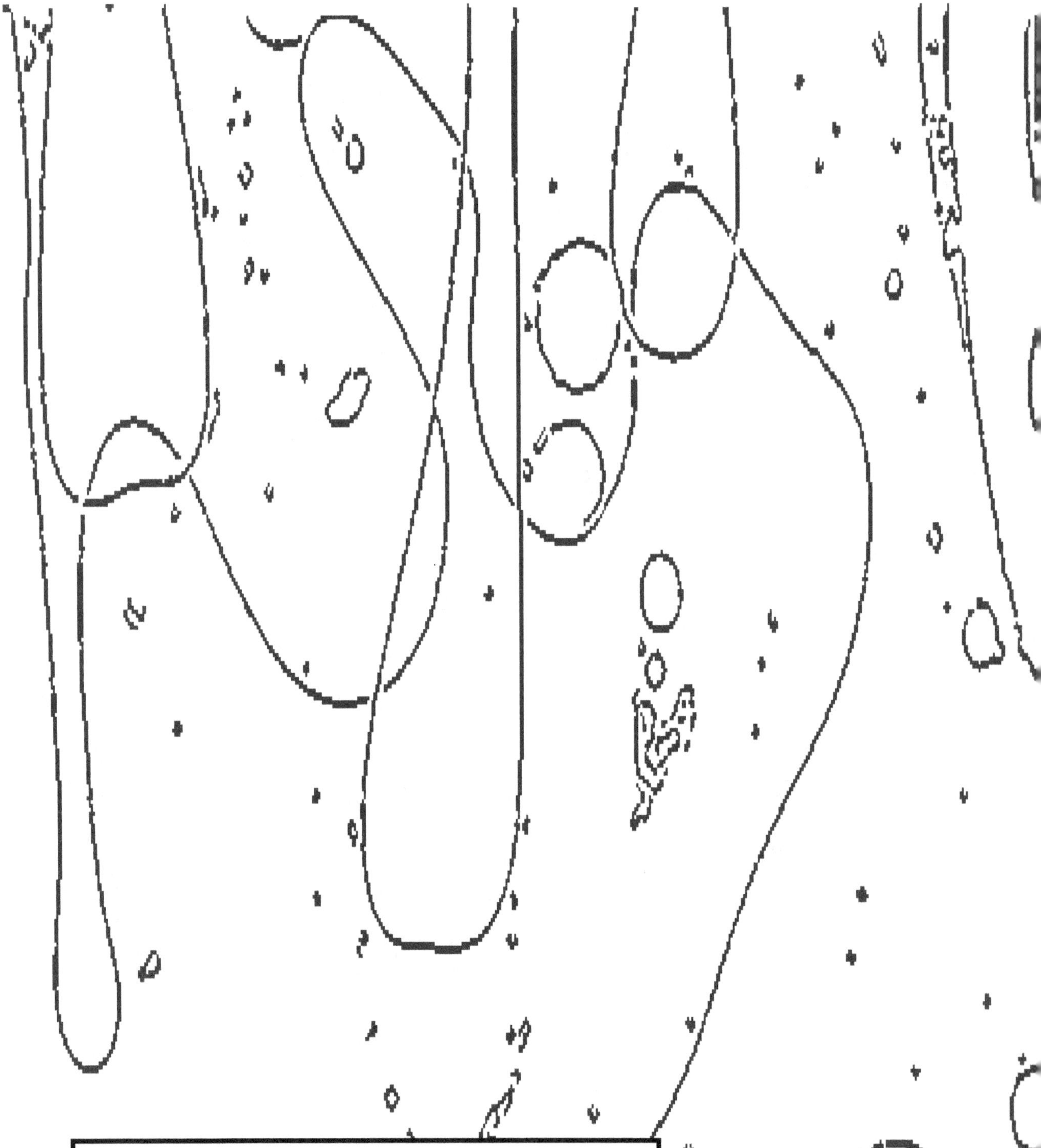

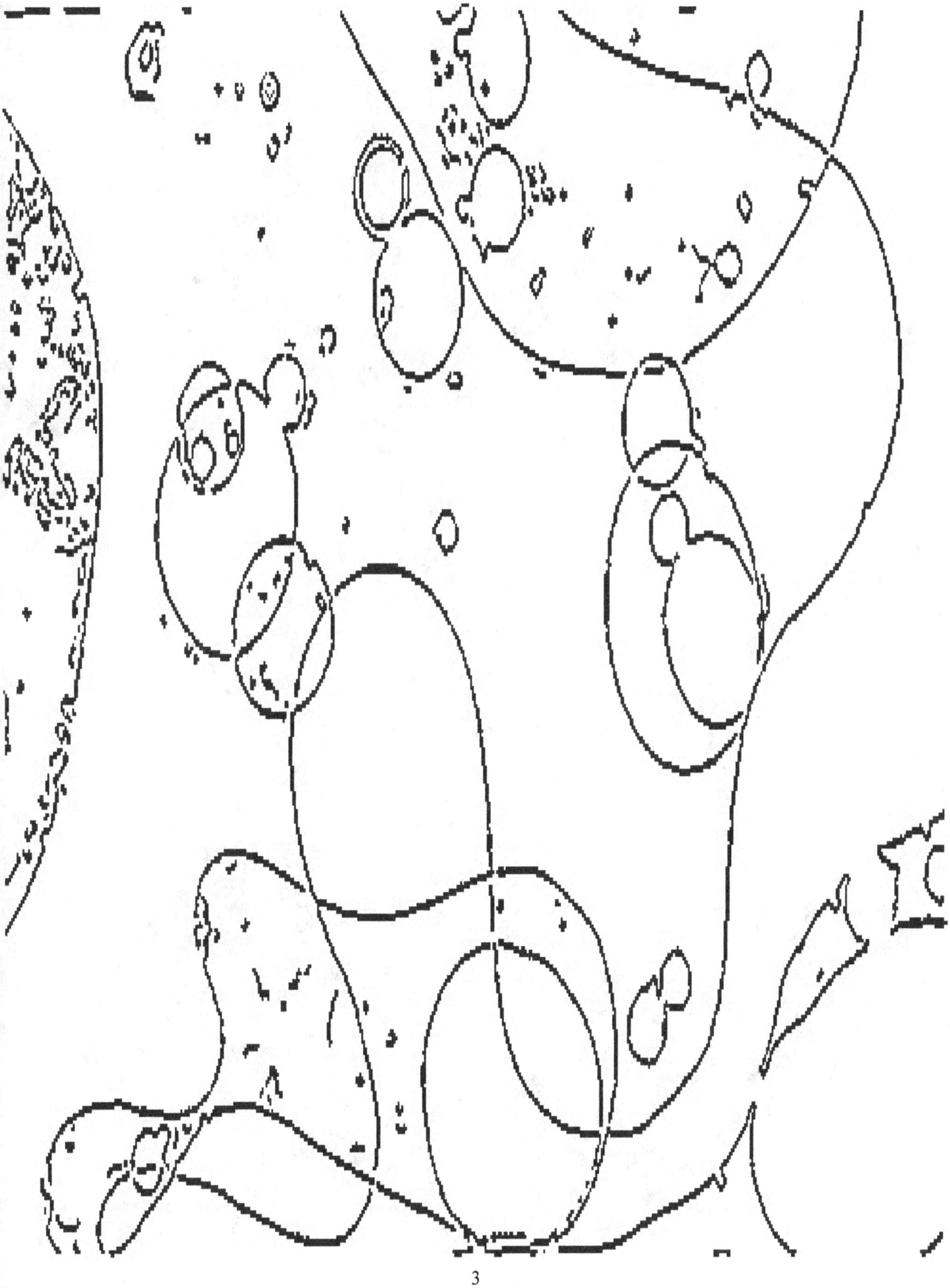

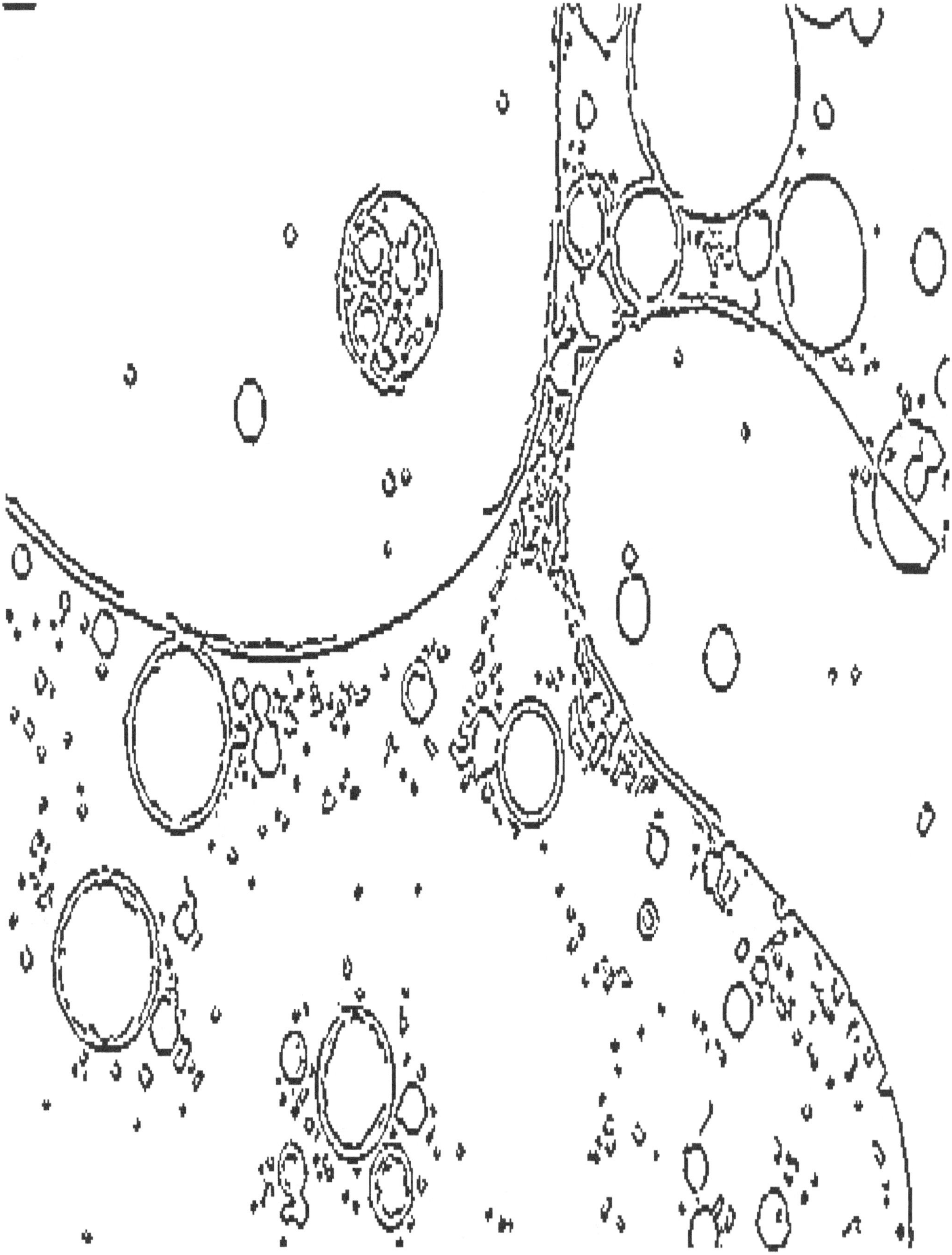

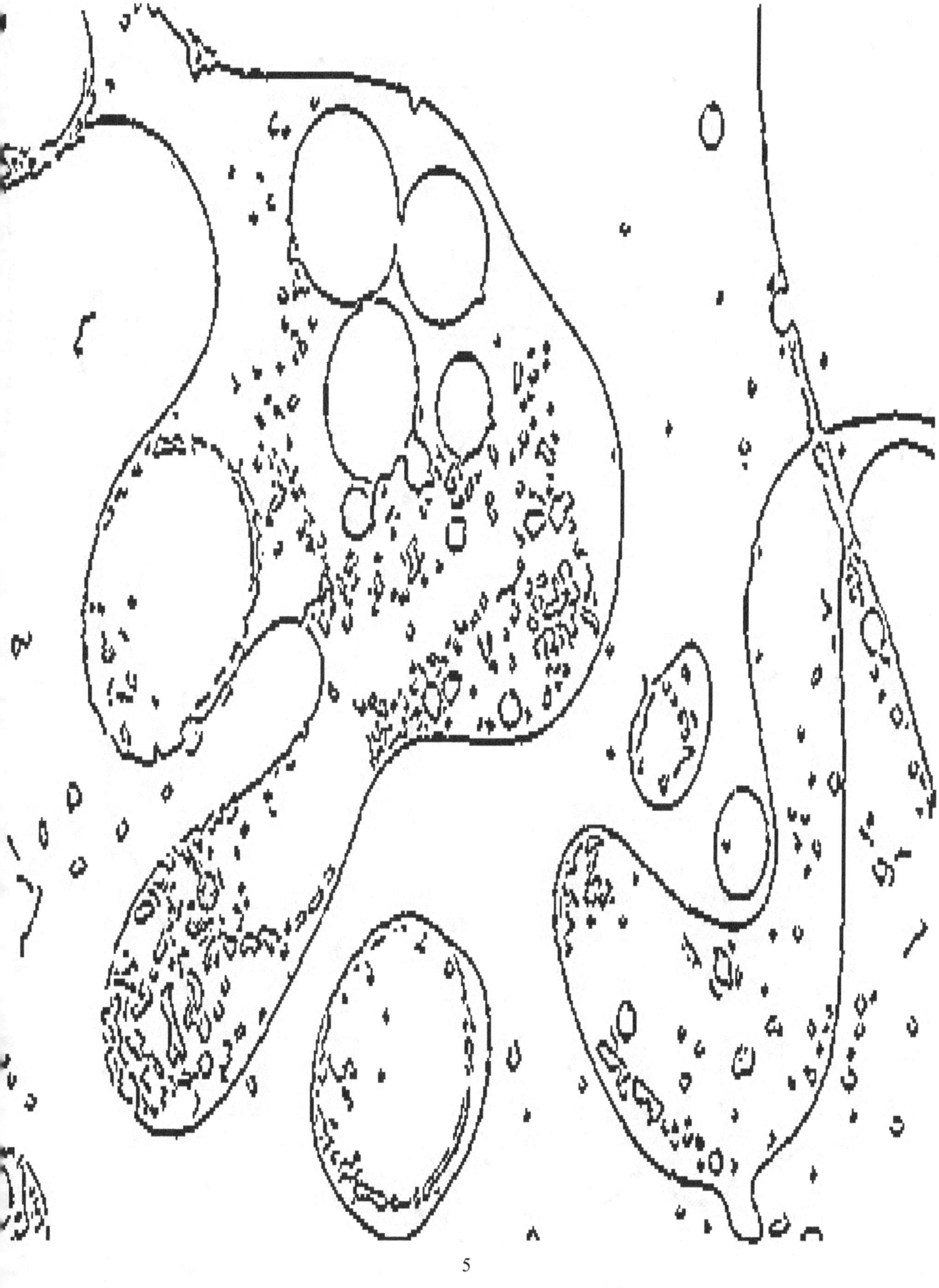

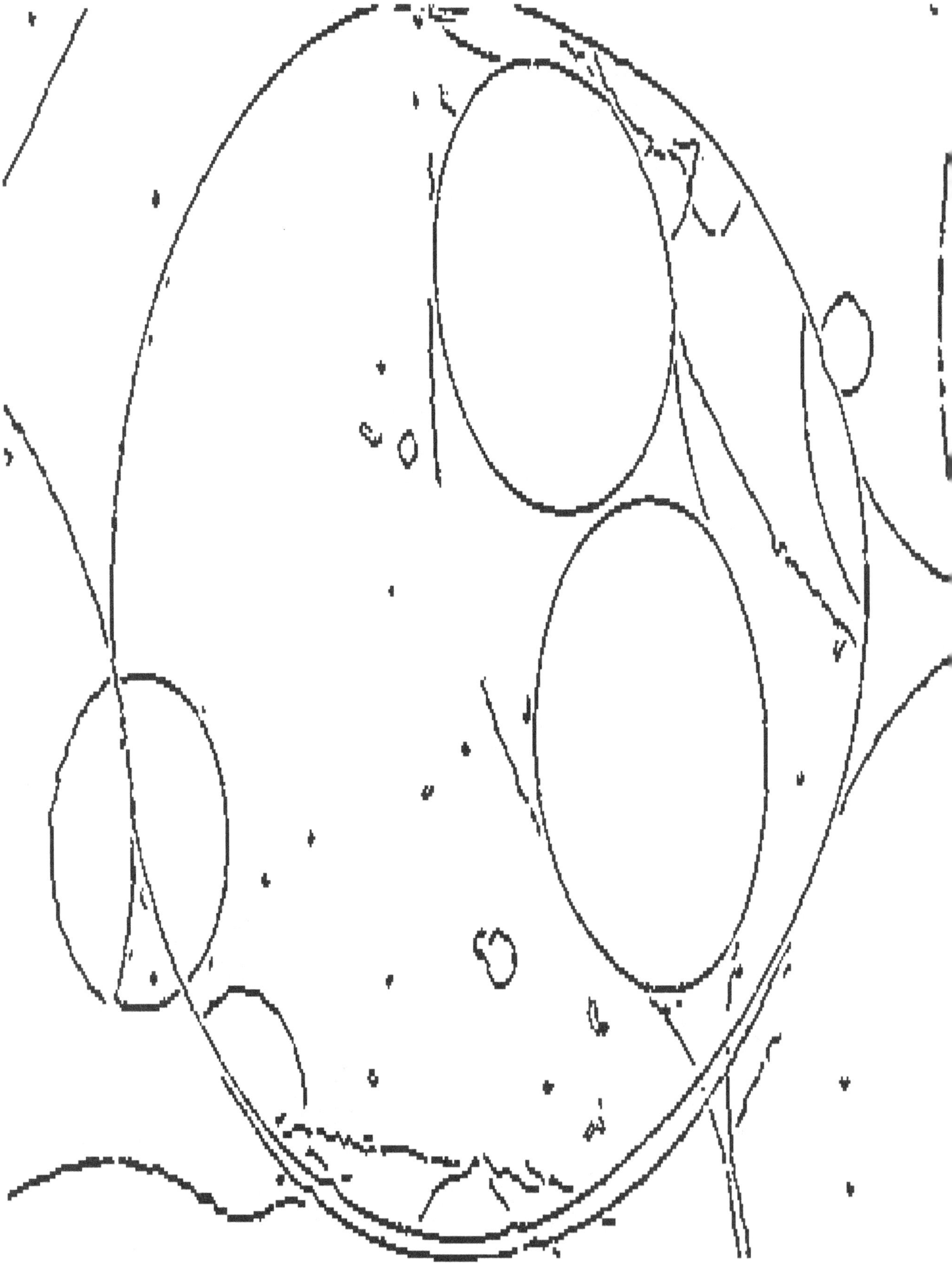

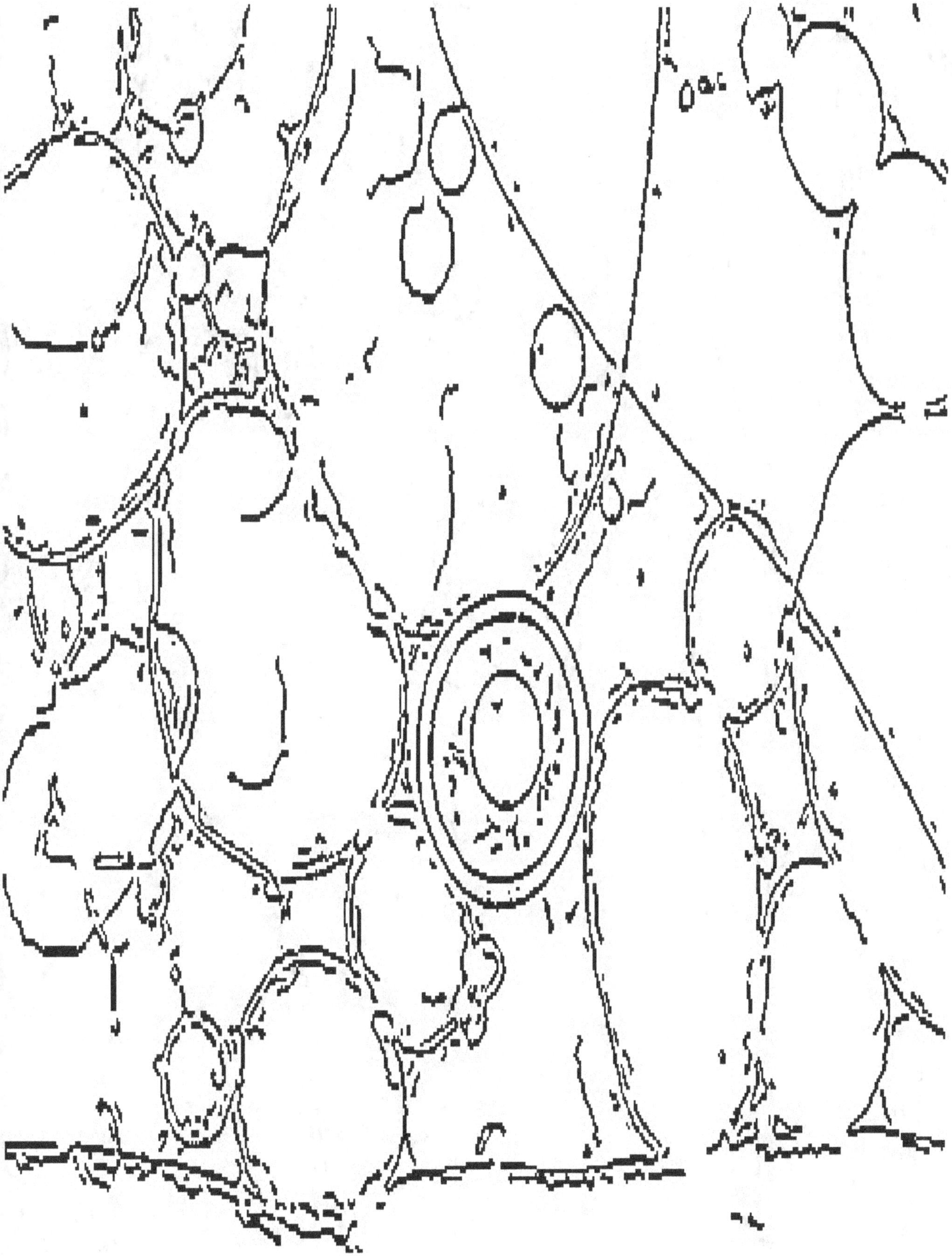

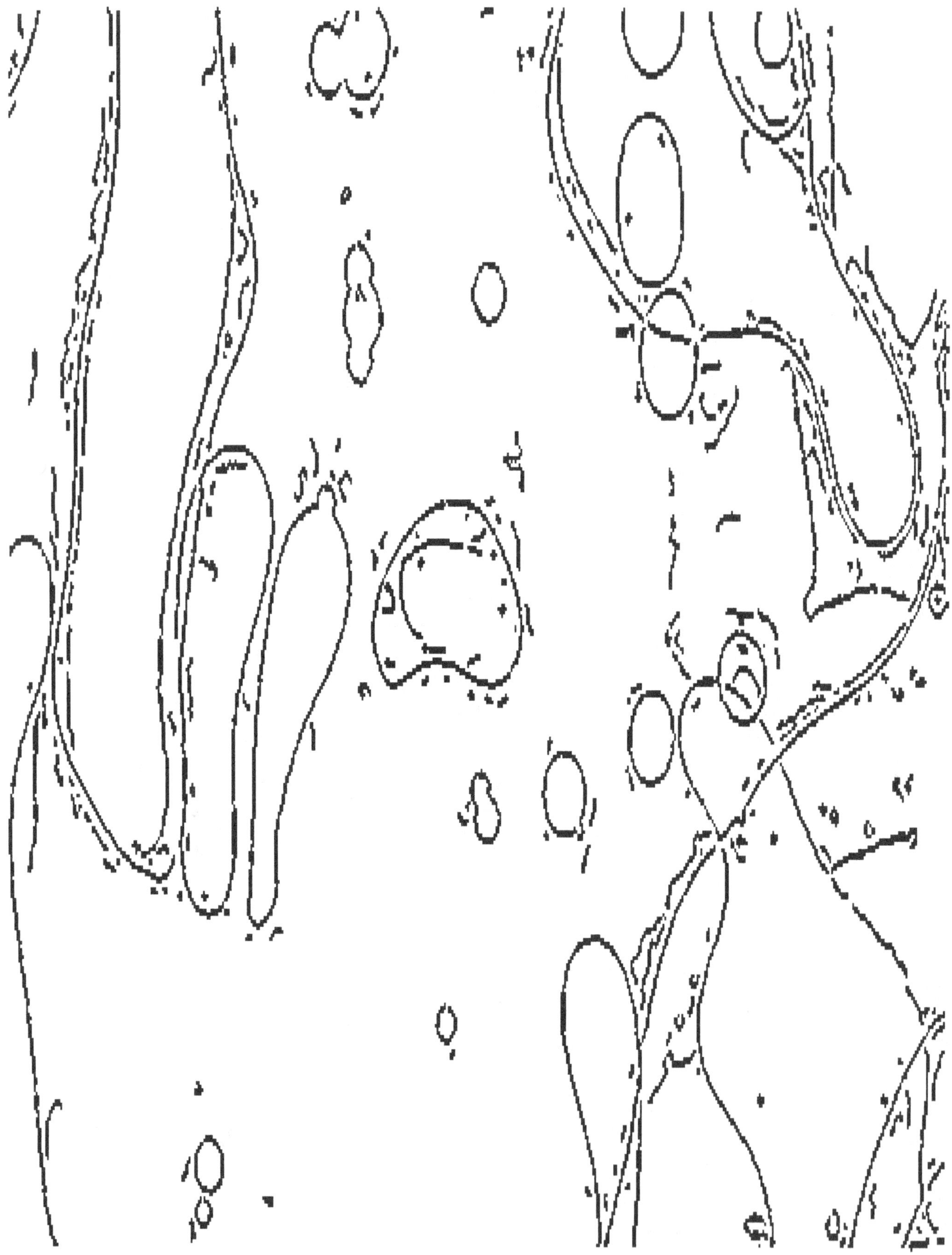

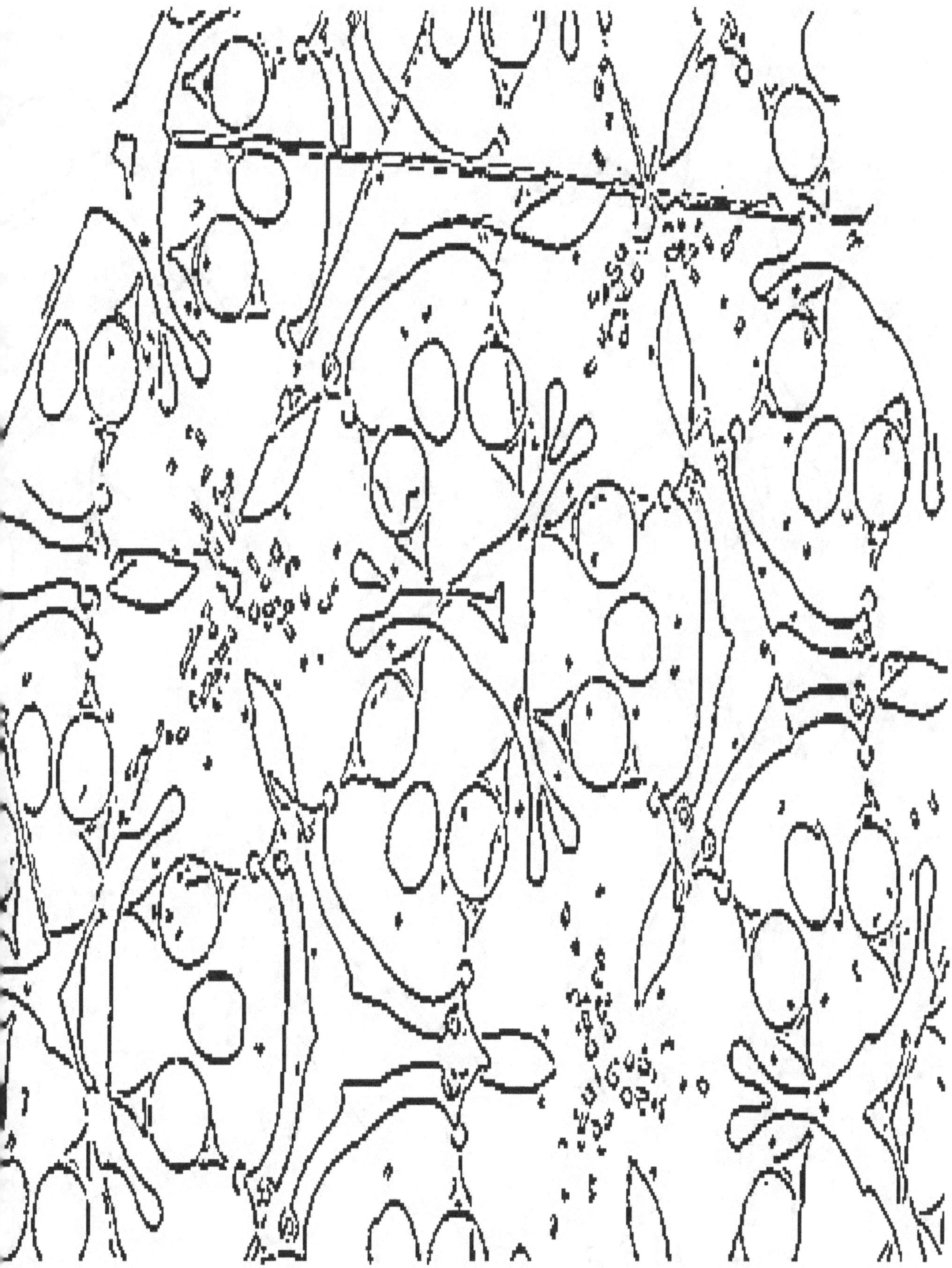

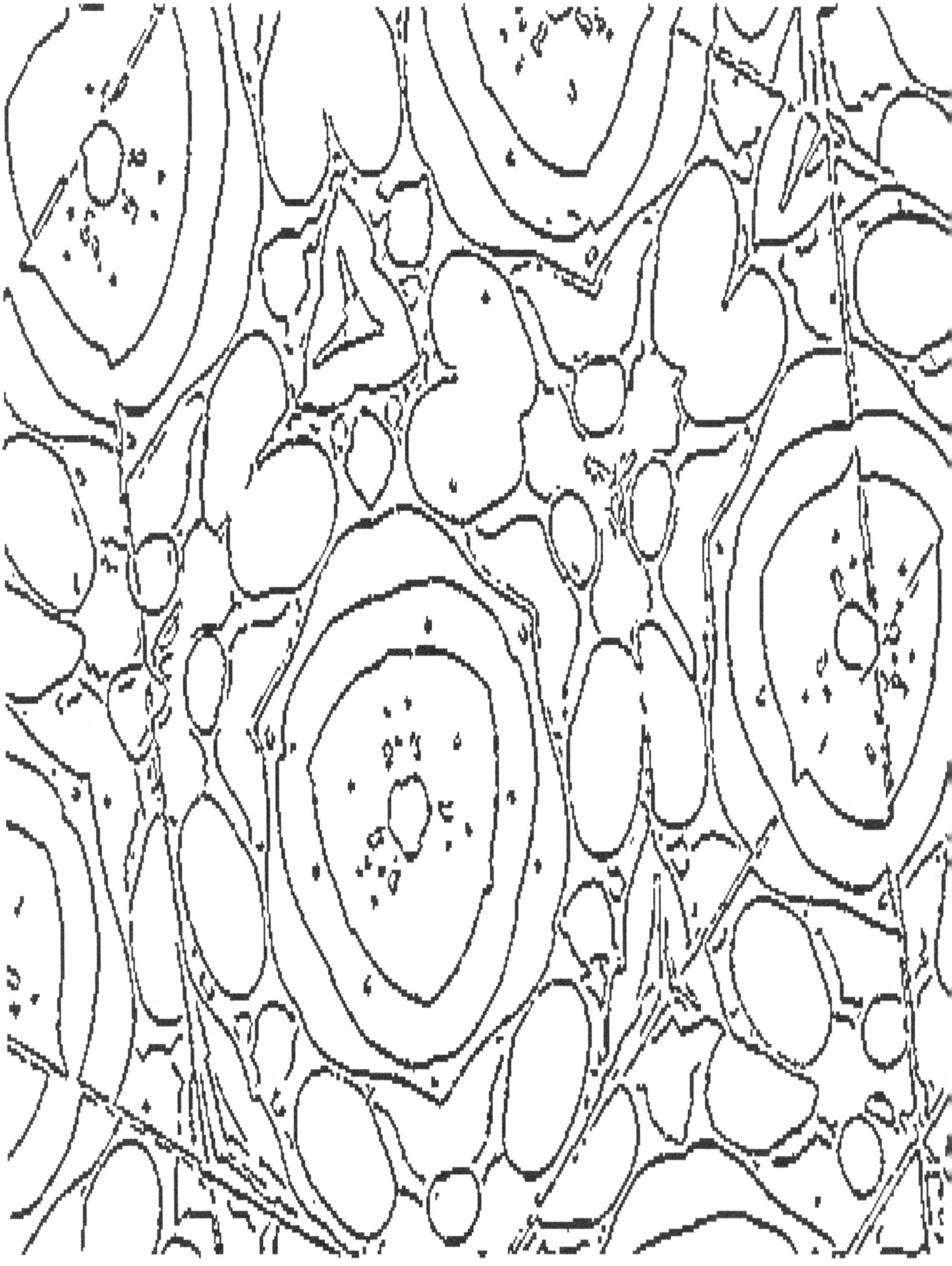

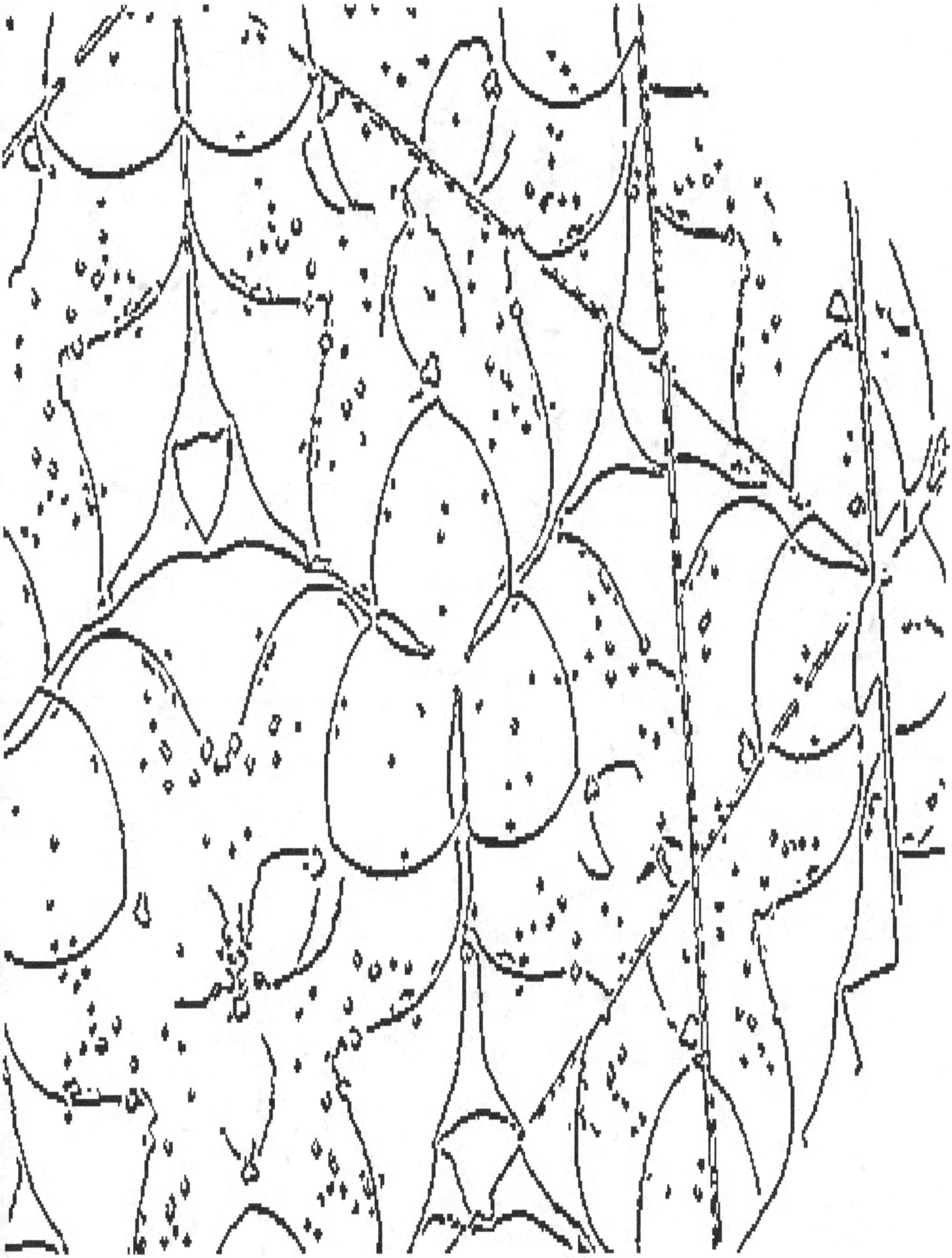

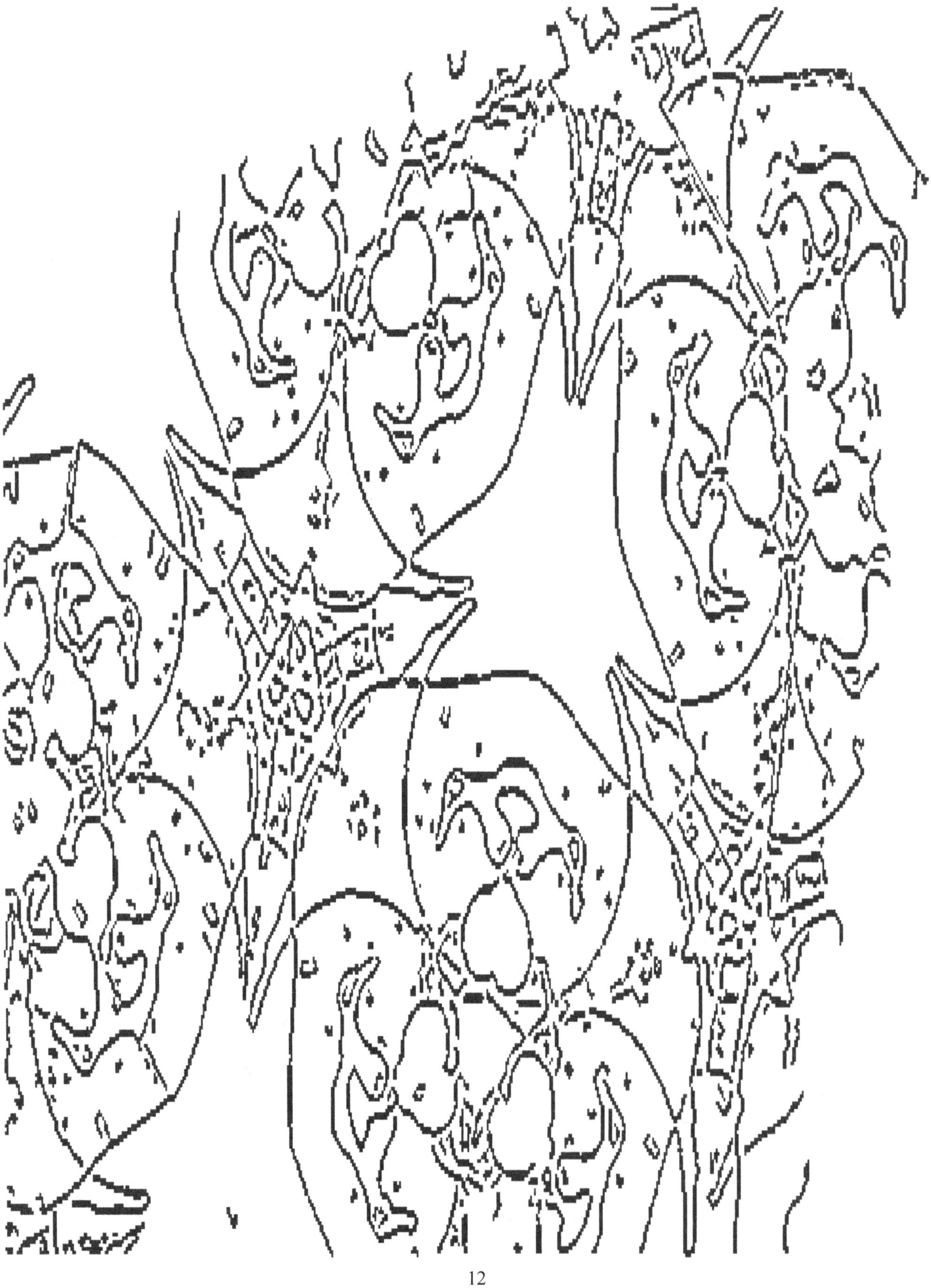

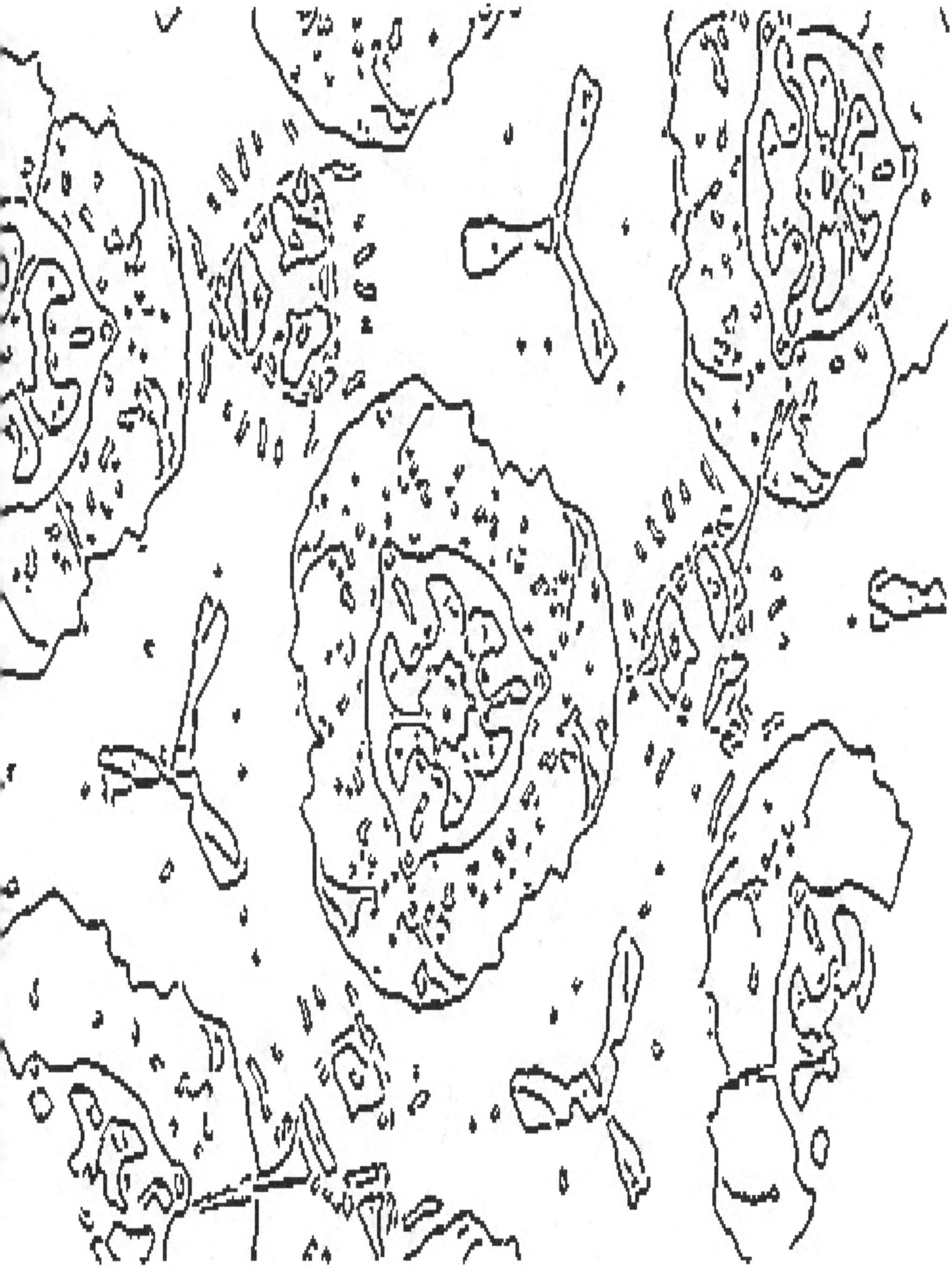

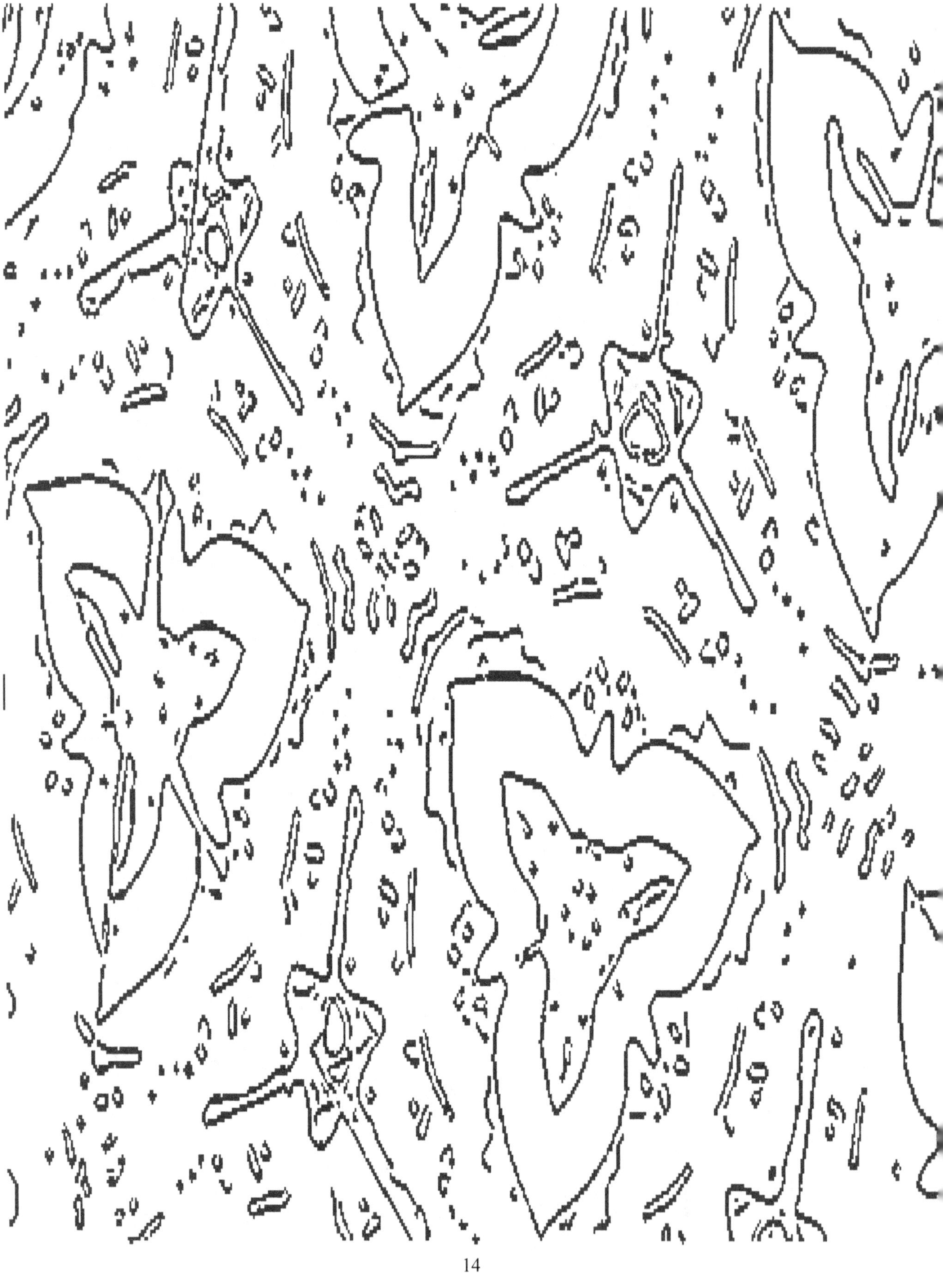

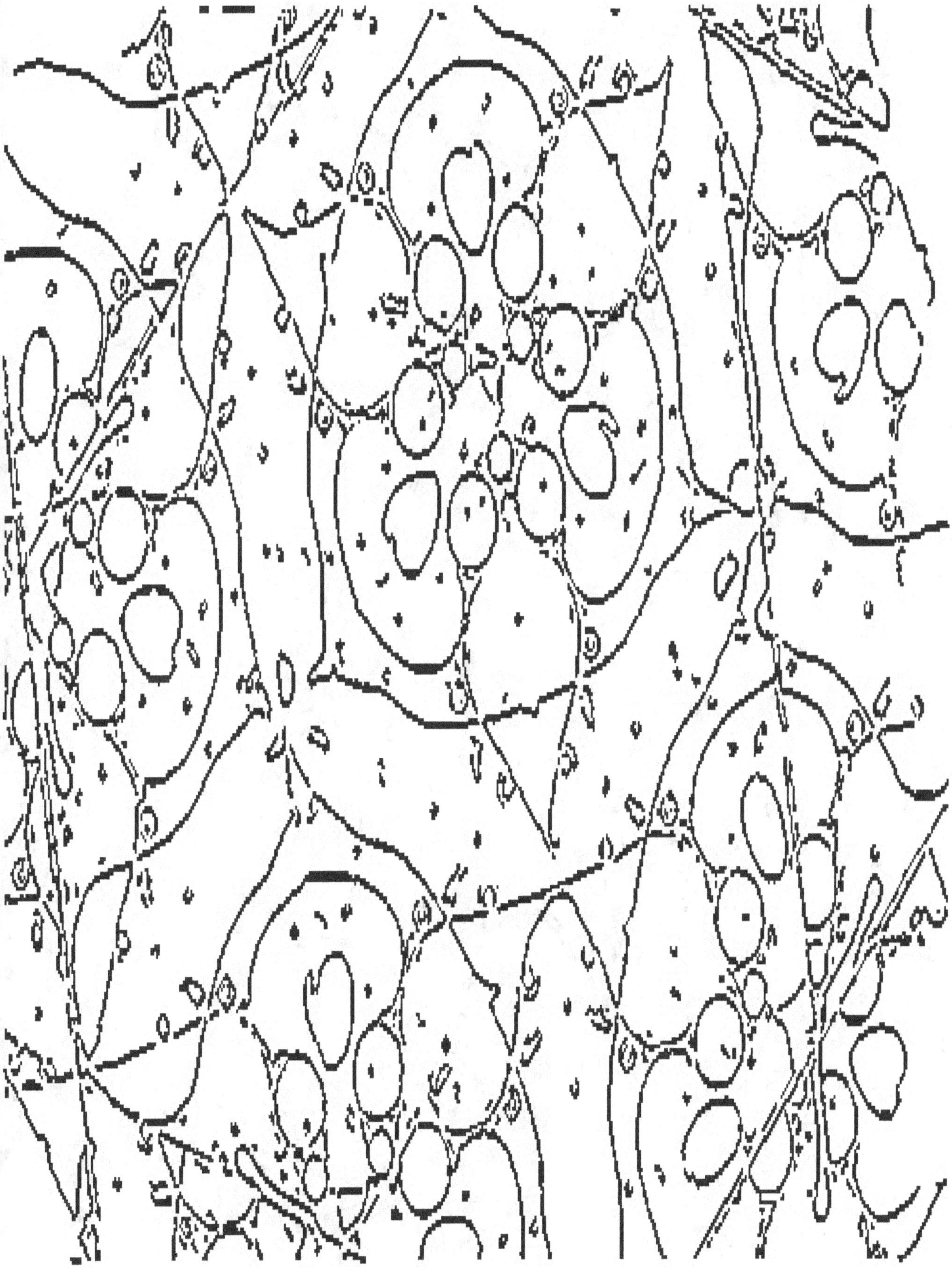

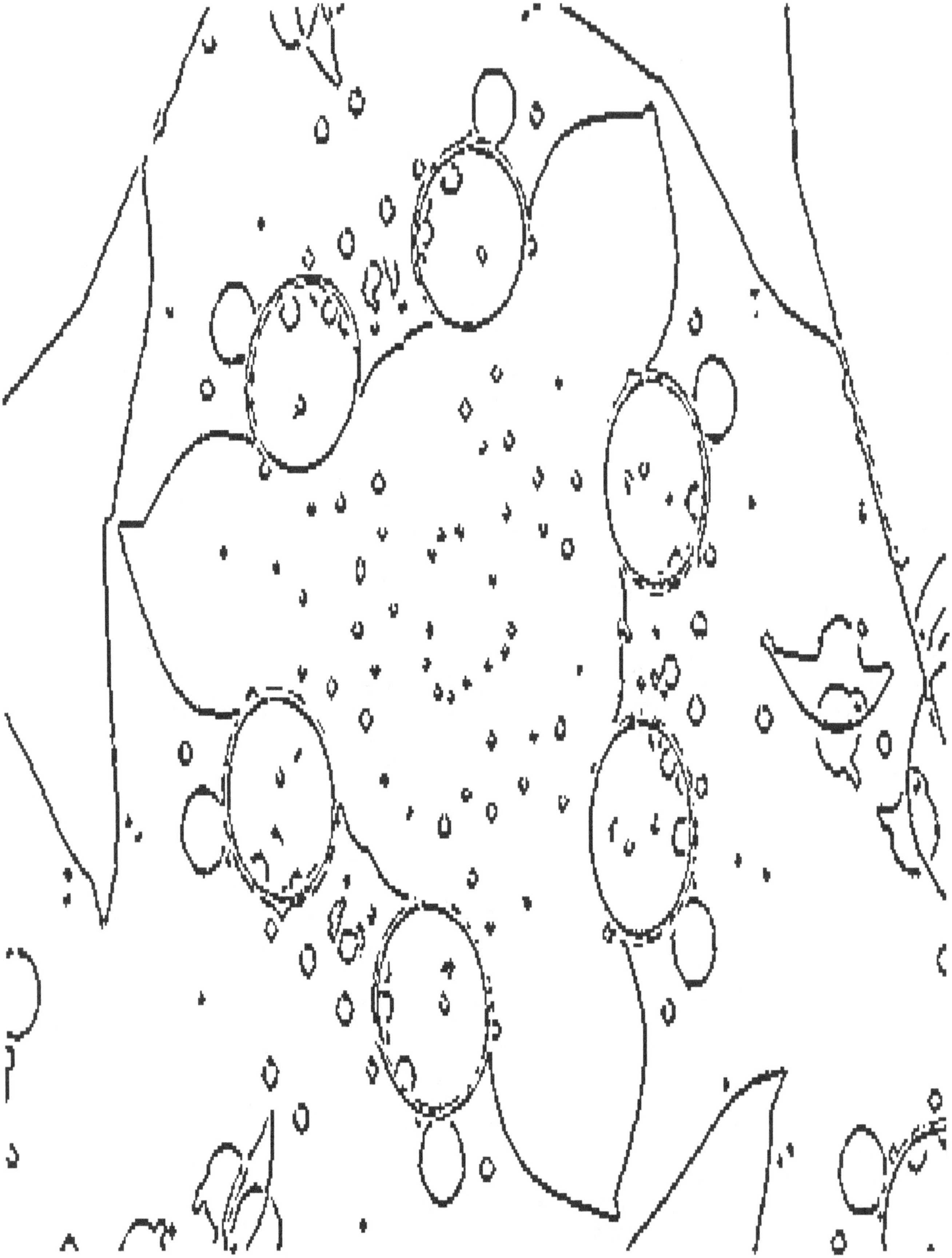

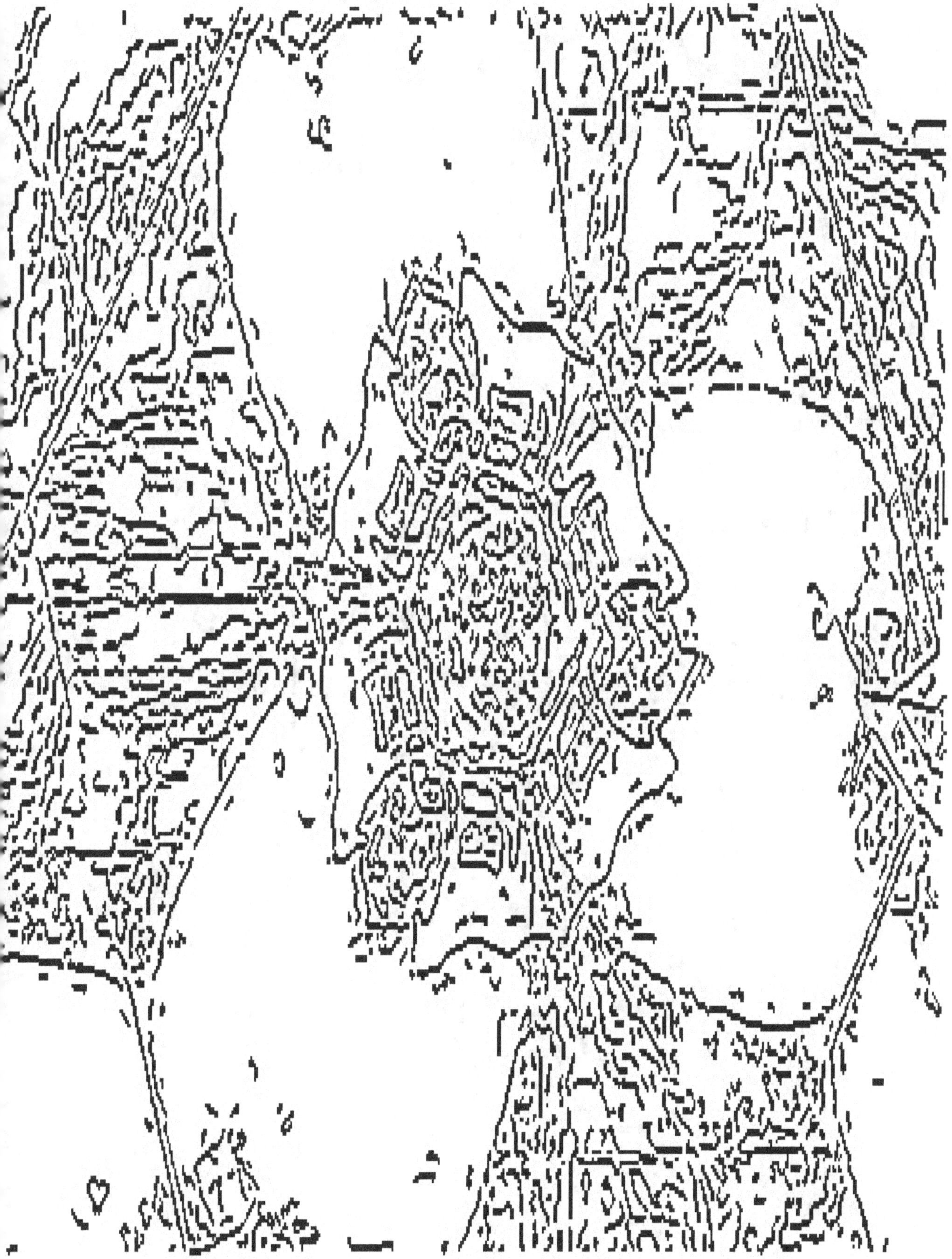

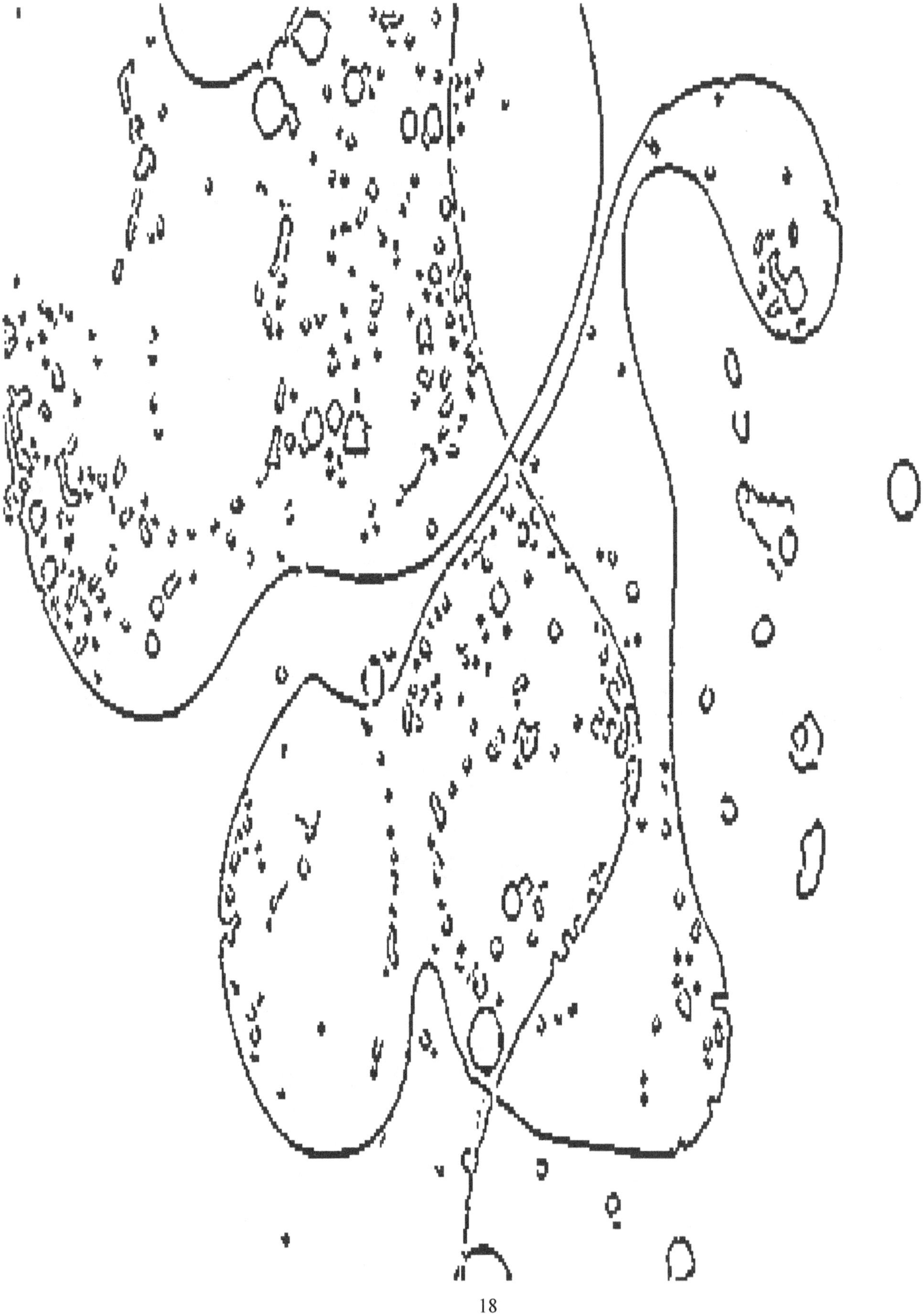

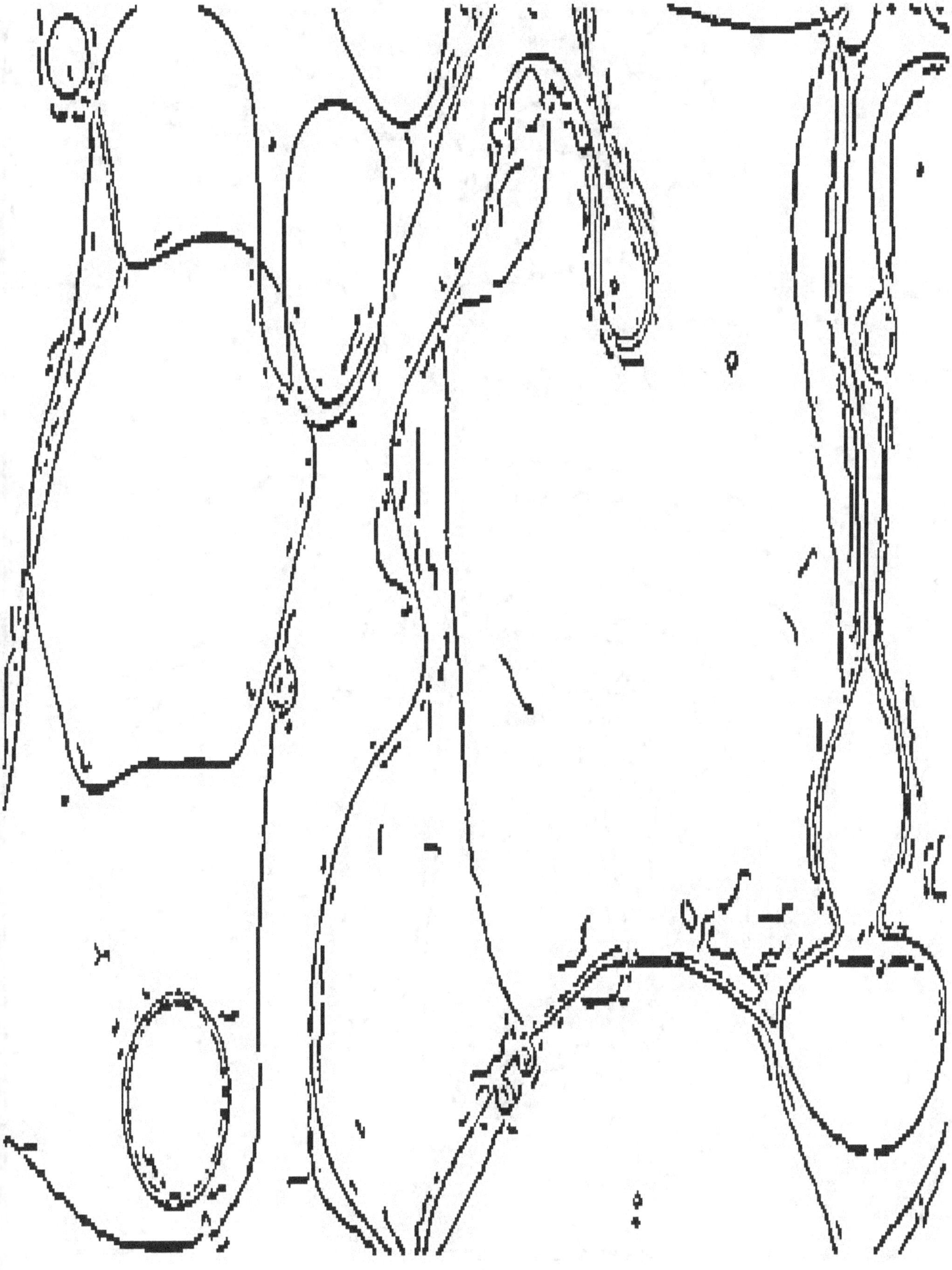

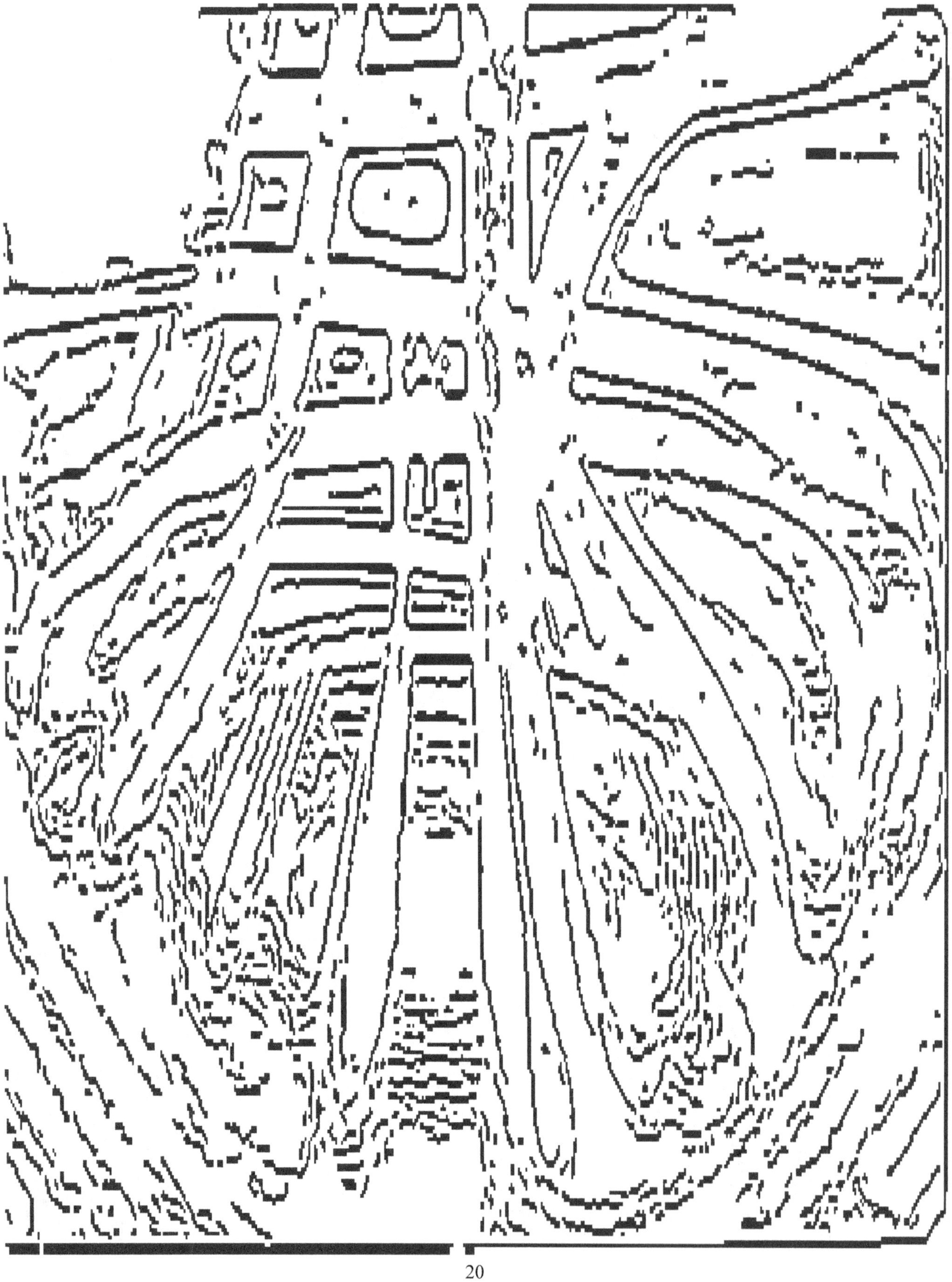

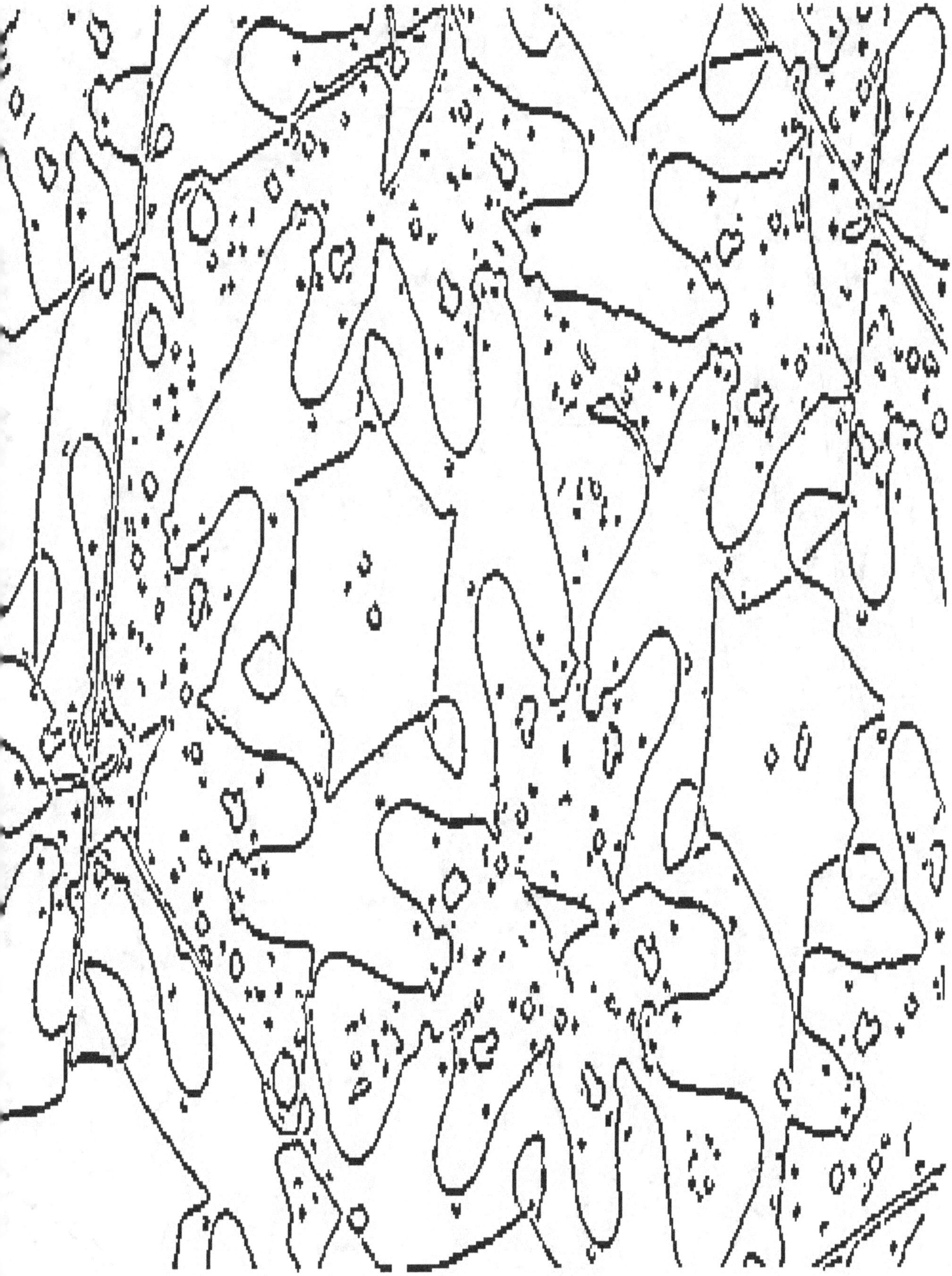

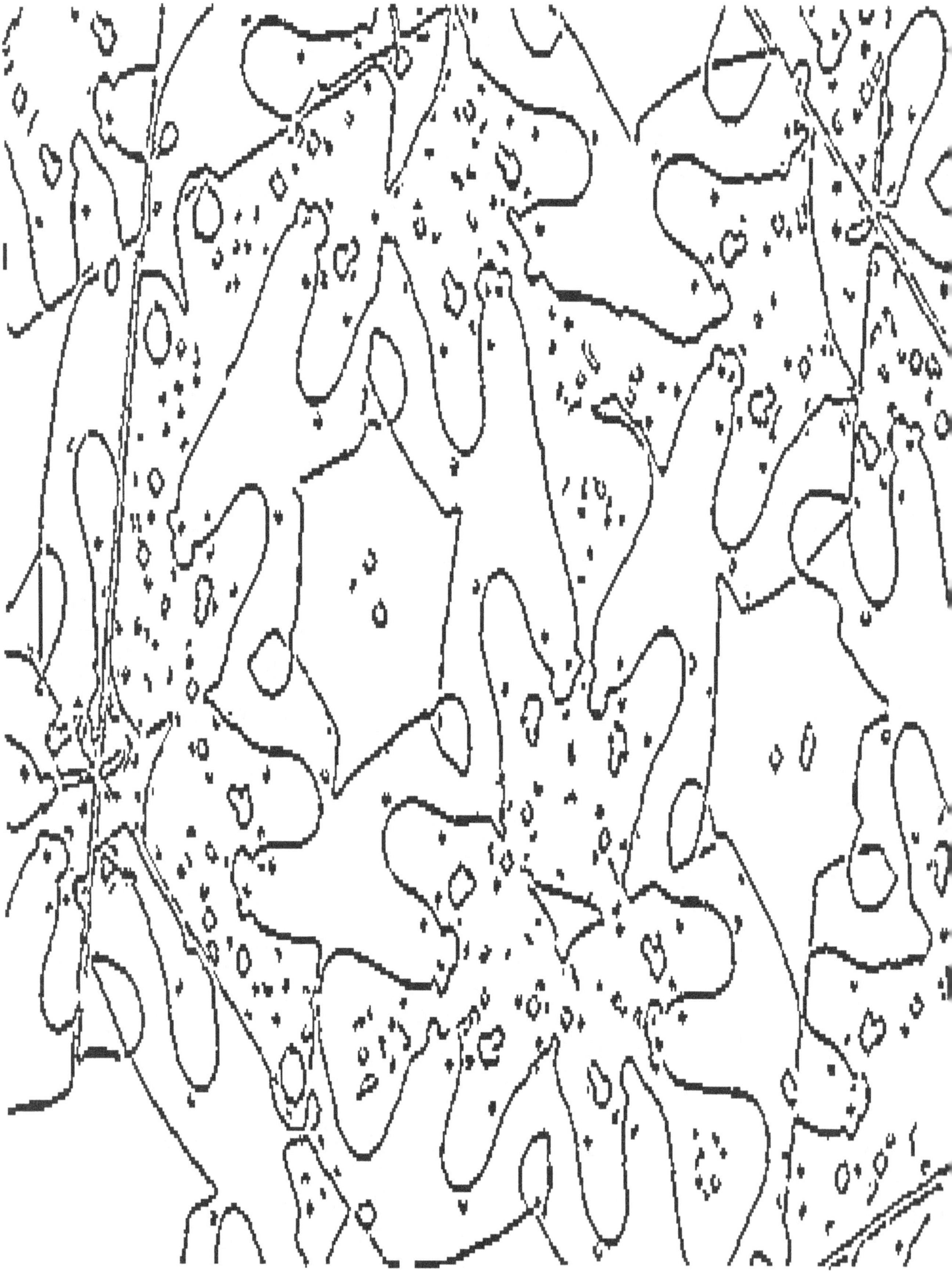

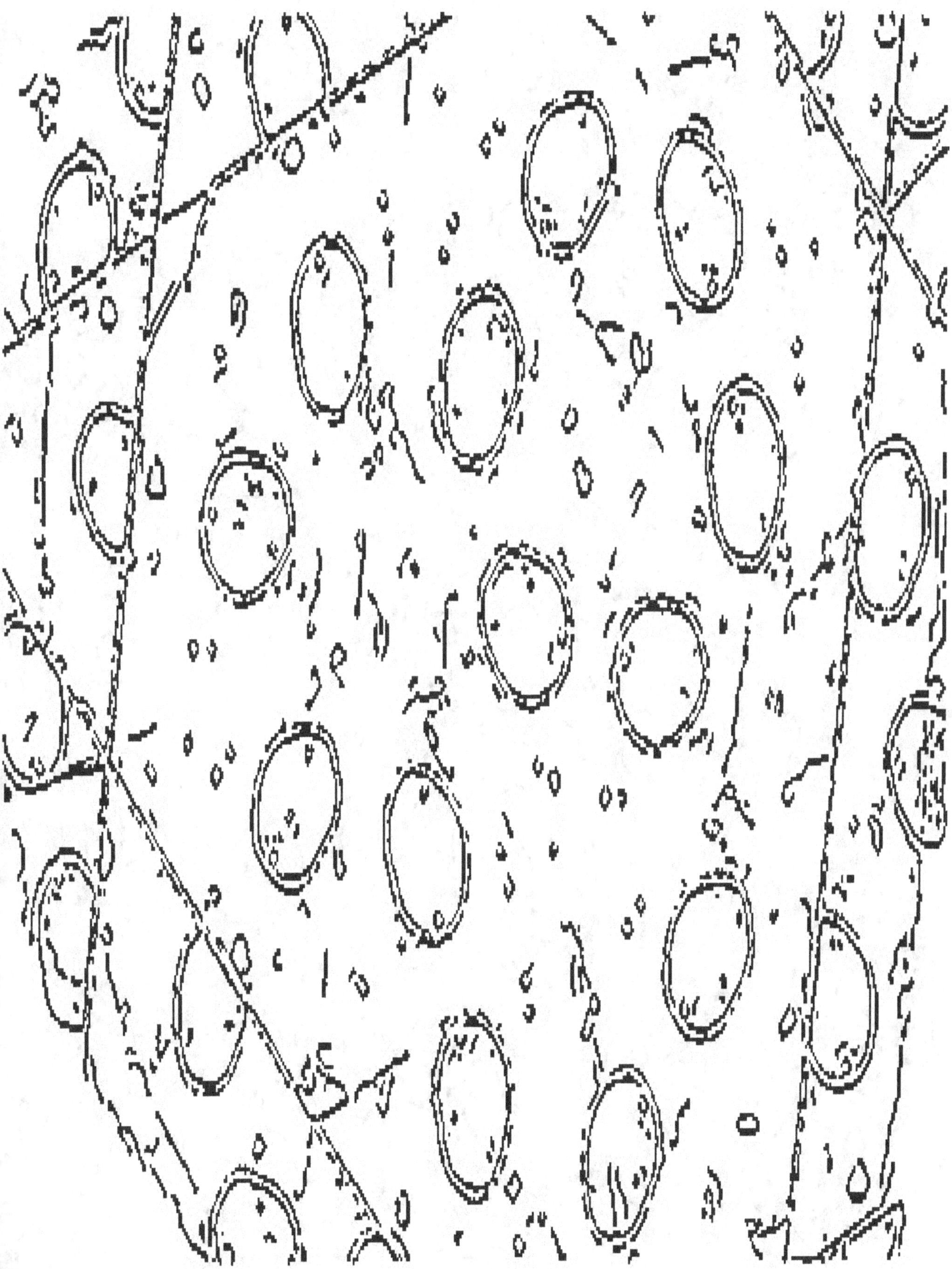

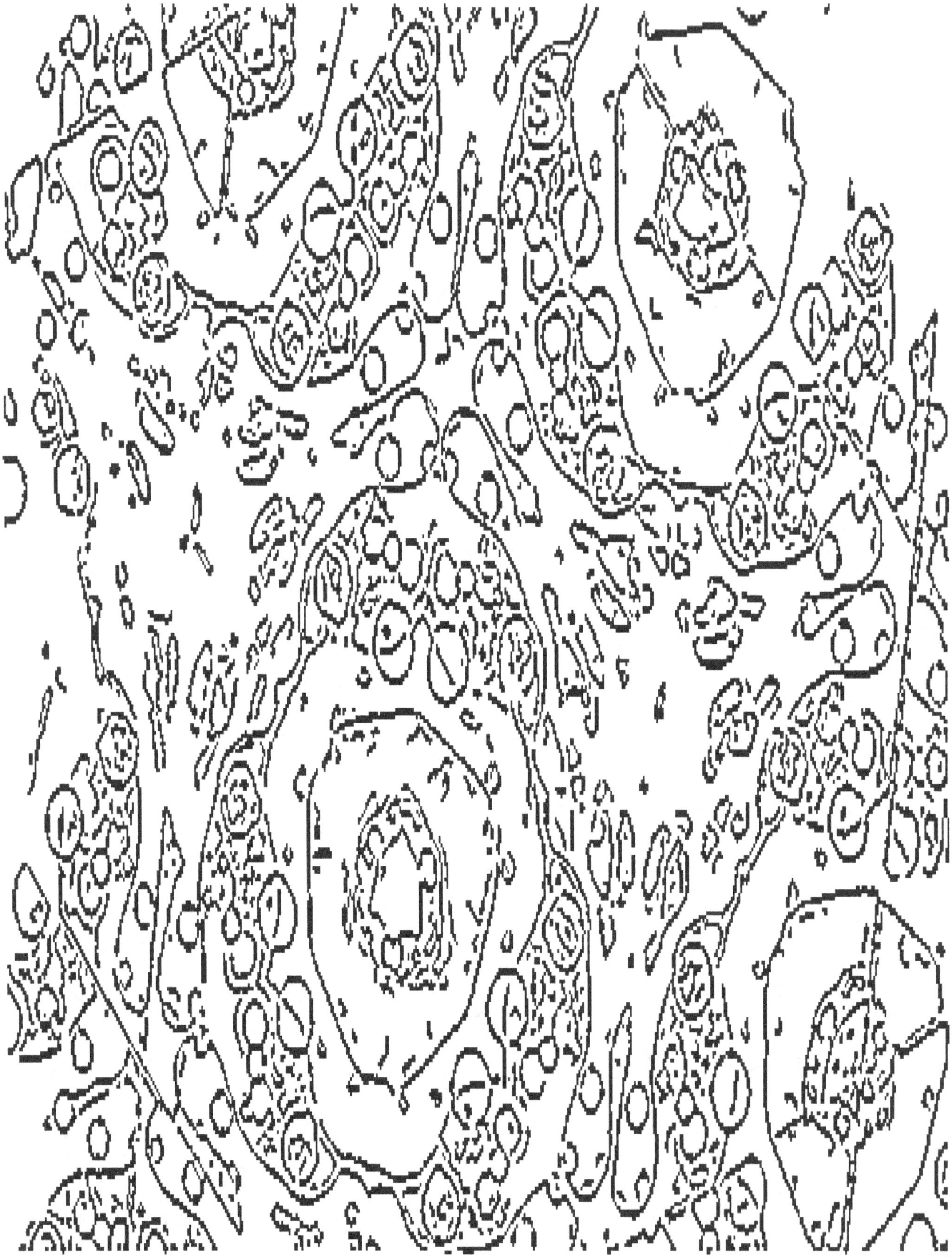

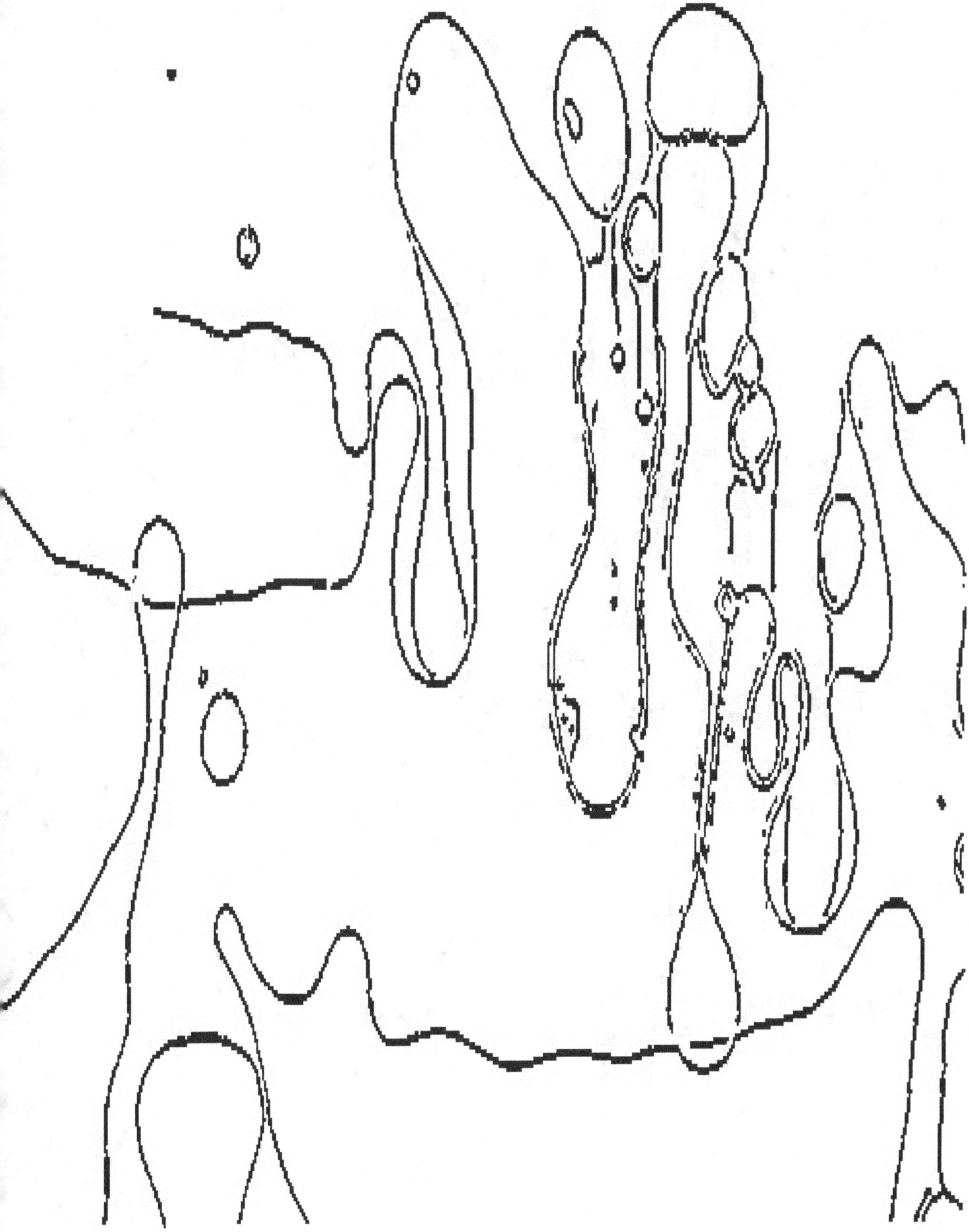

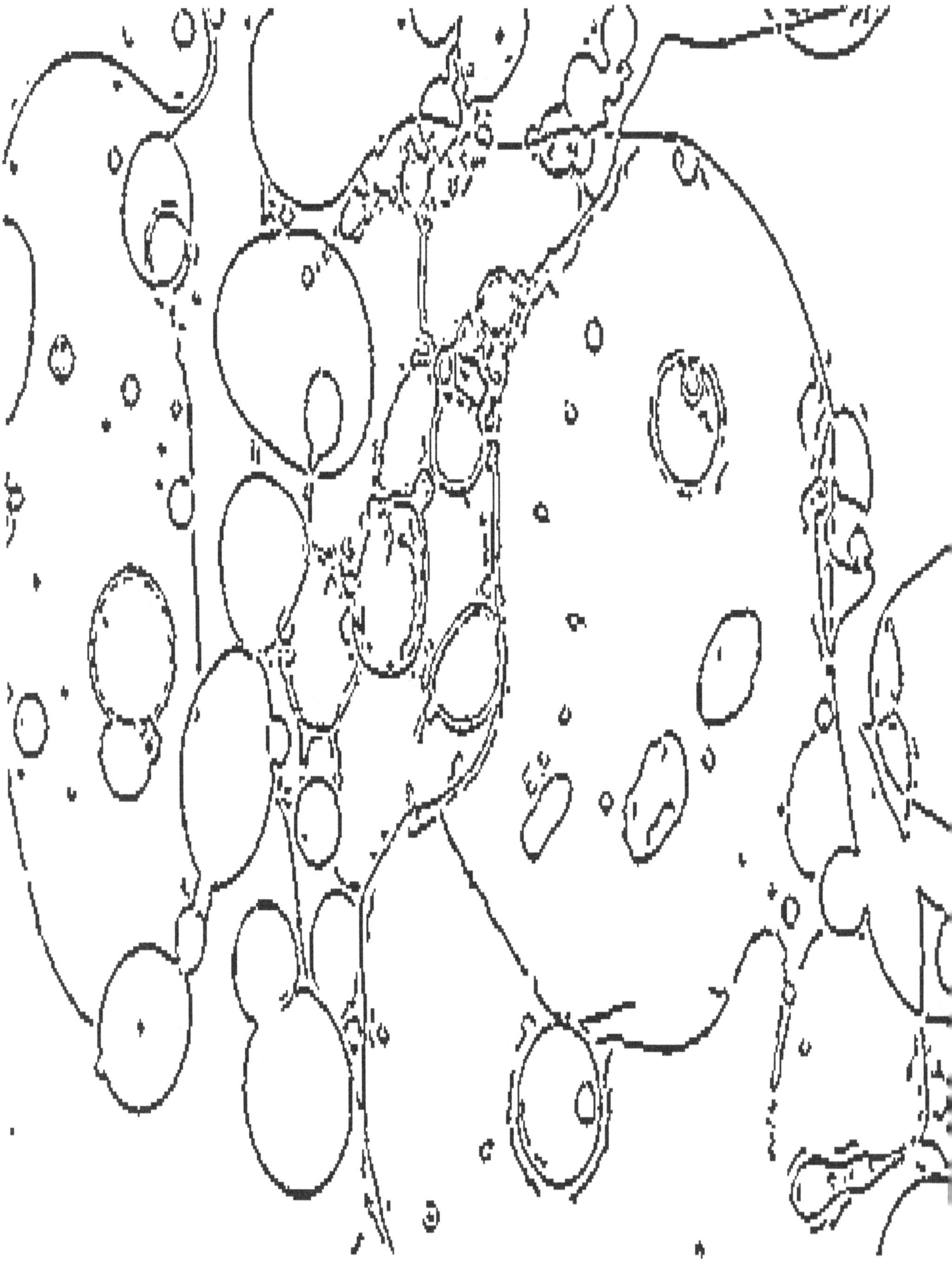

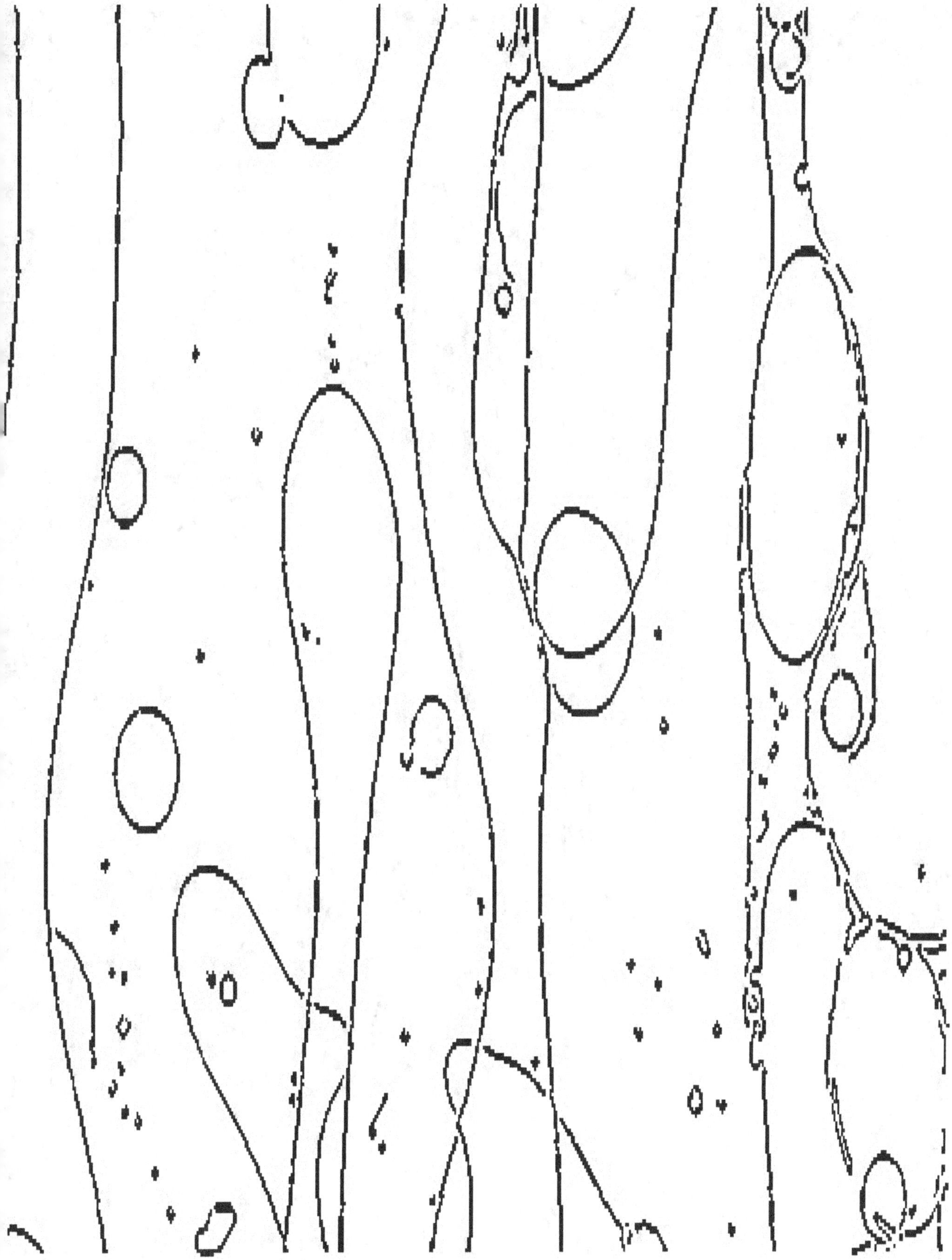

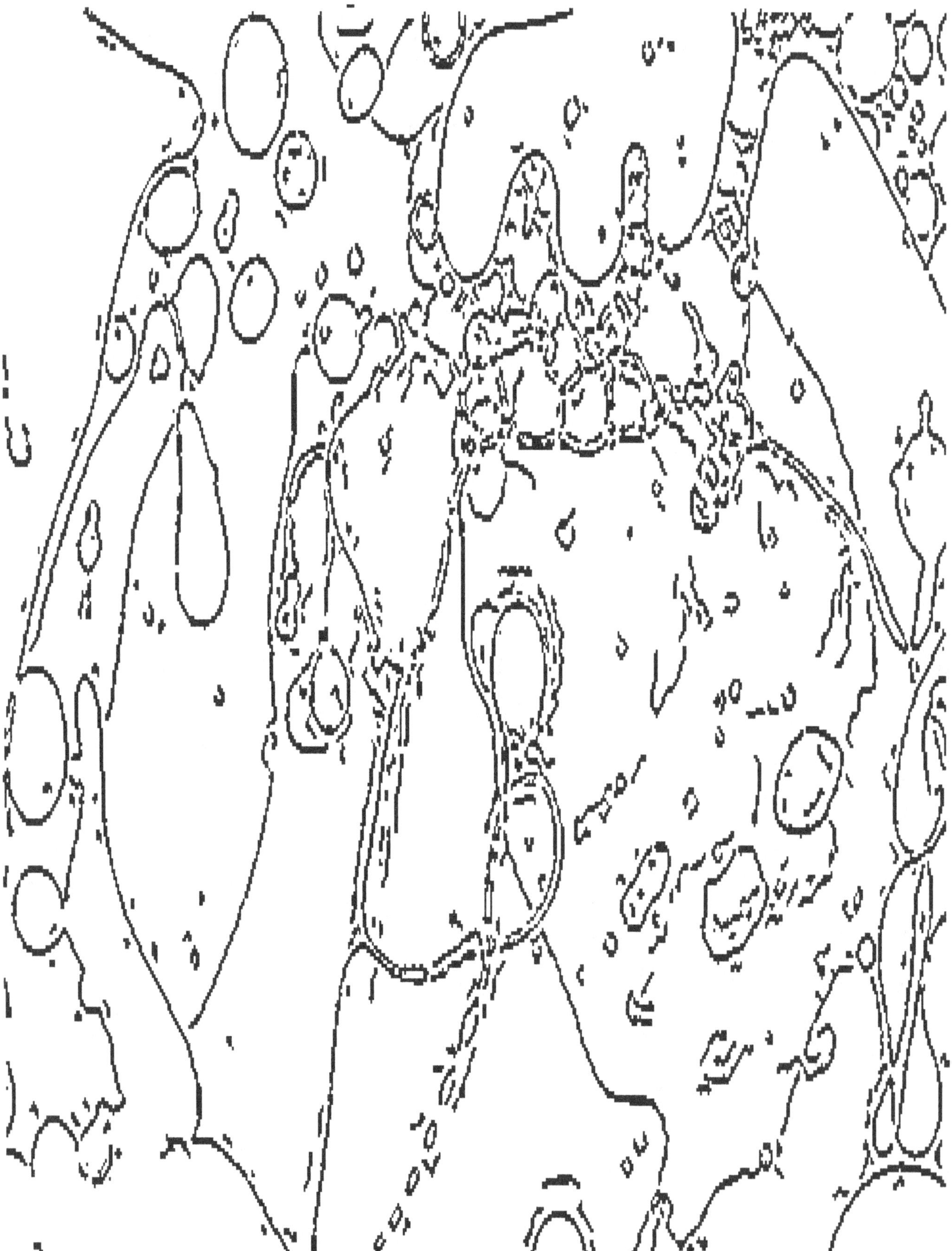

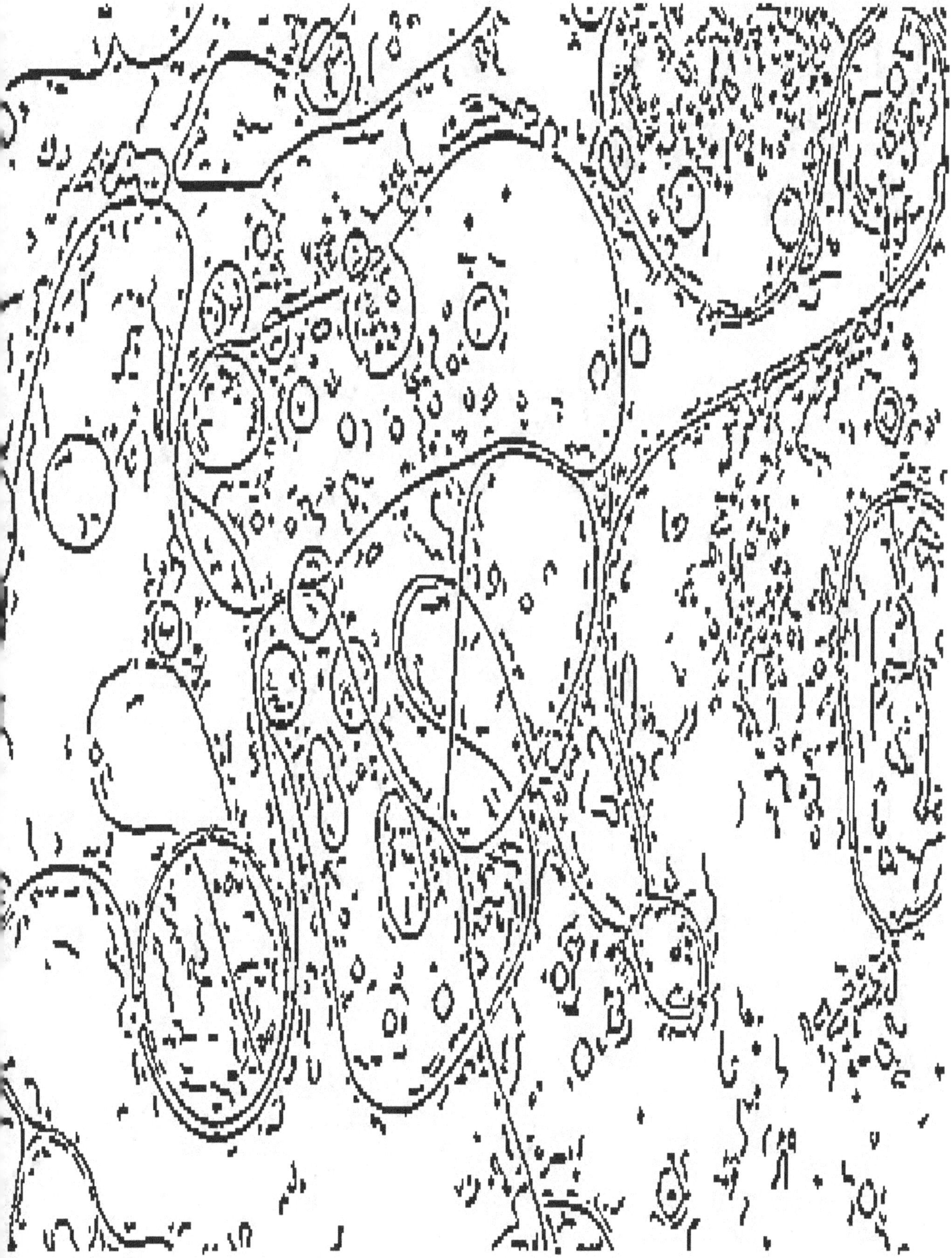

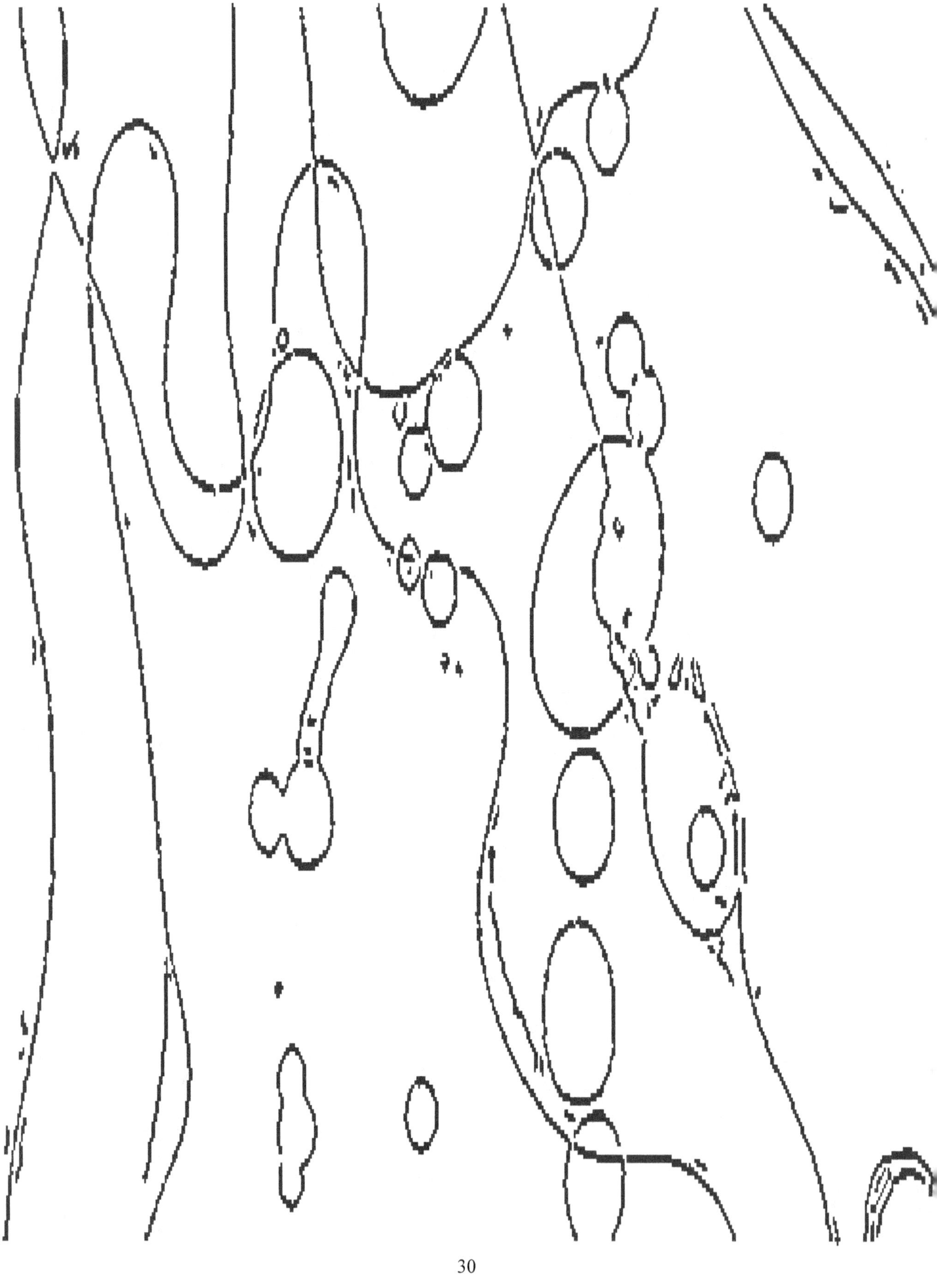

www.ingramcontent.com/pod-product-compliance
Lightning Source LLC
Chambersburg PA
CBHW081316180526
45170CB00007B/2727
* 9 7 8 1 5 2 3 4 7 4 4 4 8 *